Zoé de Las Cases

# SECRET NEW YORK

## Color Your Way to Calm

**Little, Brown and Company**

New York   Boston   London

Little, Brown and Company
Hachette Book Group
1290 Avenue of the Americas, New York, NY 10104
littlebrown.com

First North American Edition: October 2015
Originally published as *New York Secret* in France by Éditions Marabout, April 2015

Little, Brown and Company is a division of Hachette Book Group, Inc.
The Little, Brown name and logo are trademarks of Hachette Book Group, Inc.

The publisher is not responsible for websites (or their content) that are not owned by the publisher.

The Hachette Speakers Bureau provides a wide range of authors for speaking events. To find out more, go to hachettespeakersbureau.com or call (866) 376-6591.

ISBN 978-0-316-26583-6
Library of Congress Control Number: 2015944906

10 9 8 7 6 5 4

WW

Printed in the United States of America

Zoé de Las Cases is the artistic director of a creative agency in Paris.

THIS BOOK BELONGS TO:

......................................

Come In
WE'RE
OPEN

# WELCOME TO
# MY SECRET NEW YORK!

New York . . . the city of dreams! Elegant, energetic, and electrifying, this city of creativity and ambition always offers something new to discover. From the sprawling avenues of Manhattan to the eclectic neighborhoods of Brooklyn, a New York in black and white is just waiting for you and your colored pencils to bring it to life.

After a walk on the High Line, board the Staten Island Ferry to view the magnificent skyline and glimpse the Statue of Liberty. Lose yourself among the flashing lights of Times Square. See a Broadway show. Become a child again at Coney Island's Luna Park. Enjoy the delicious specialties of Little Italy before heading west and getting lost in the bustling crowds of Chelsea Market. At nightfall, sit at a café and people watch in the beautiful West Village.

Forget your stress and bring the Big Apple to life! Reveal your inner artist and give free rein to your imagination as you let the spirit of New York be your guide.

DETOX
BIO
AB

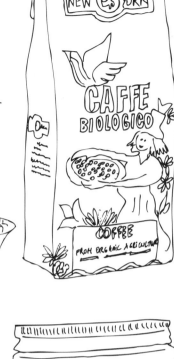

NEW YORK
CAFFE
BIOLOGICO
COFFEE
FROM ORGANIC AGRICULTURE

PUKCO
chamomile
& vanilla
ORGANIC HERBAL
TEA

ARGAN
Oil

ARGAN
Oil

OLiViA

Puressentiel
BOIS DE ROSE
D'ASIE
1
ORGANIC OIL
PURE &
NATURAL
JILA PURE ESSENCE

Puressentiel
1
OIL IN MORE

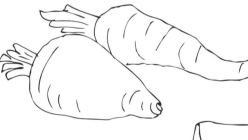

Clearspring
ORGANIC
TOFU
FIRM & SILKEN
LIGHT | LOW FAT | DAIRY FREE | GLUTEN FREE

PRIMÉAL
Graines de
lin doré
AB
250g

ADULT / ADULTE
NATURAL
1
LARGE BREED

NATURAL
1
Adulte

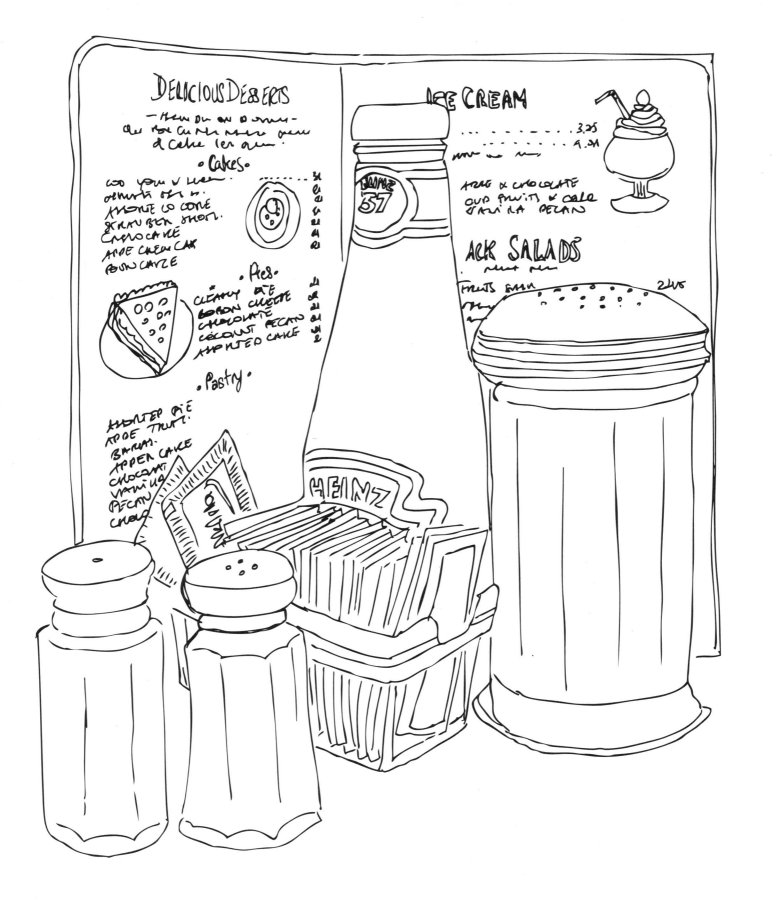

# Central Park Lower Loop

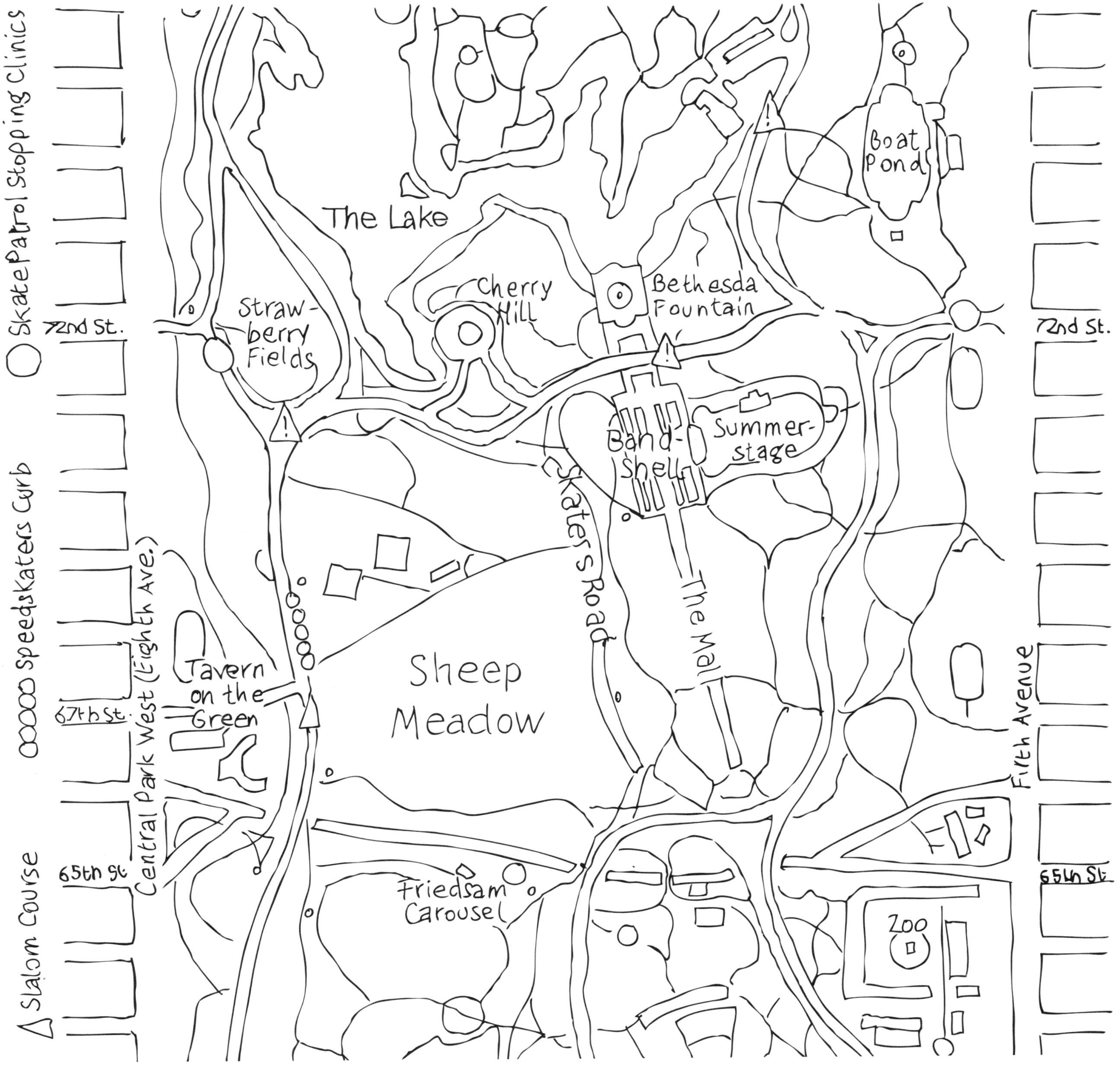

Skate Patrol Stopping Clinics

○ Skate Patrol Stopping Clinics

⊙⊙⊙⊙ Speedskaters Curb

△ Slalom Course

72nd St.

72nd St.

67th St.

65th St.

Central Park West (Eighth Ave.)

Fifth Avenue

72nd St.

65th St.

The Lake

Strawberry Fields

Cherry Hill

Bethesda Fountain

Boat Pond

Band-shell

Summer-stage

Skater's Road

The Mall

Tavern on the Green

Sheep Meadow

Friedsam Carousel

Zoo

NEW YORK

New York

NEW YORK

NEW YORK

Welcome to

# Central Park

For further information on the Park please contact:

**Park Office 638 56081**

Carder/Ranger 69-1458

Community Patrol 666 5865

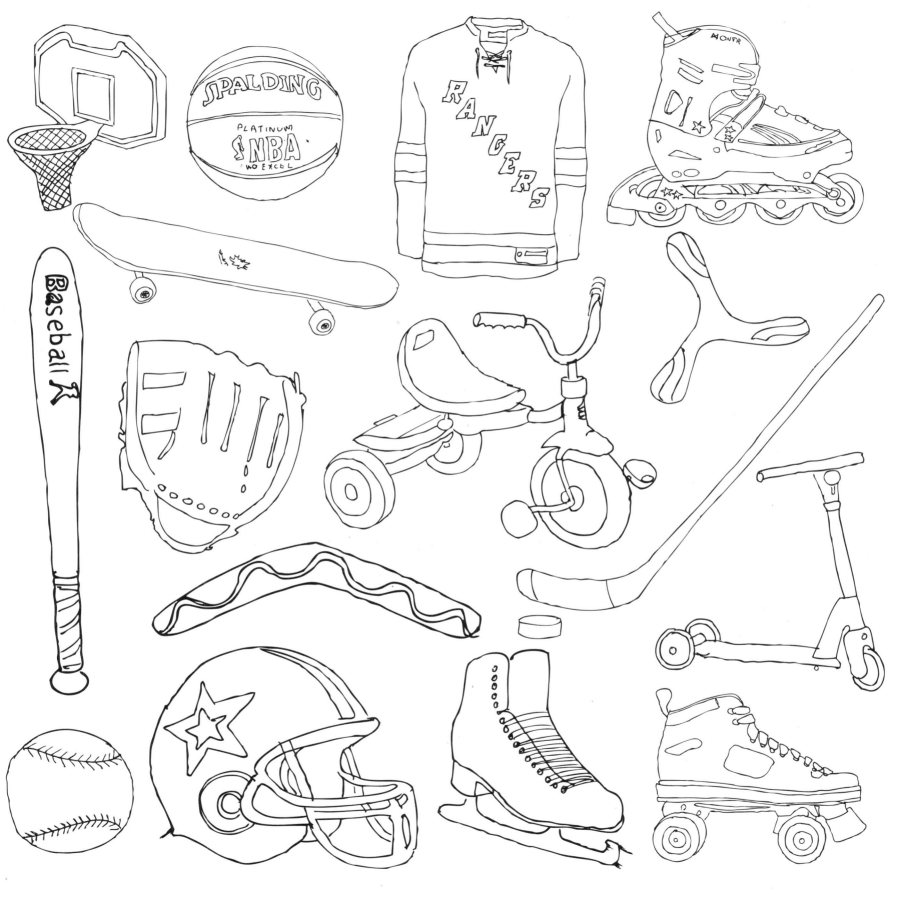

# BIKE like a NEW YORKER.

# NEW YORK, I LOVE YOU.

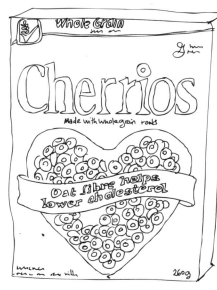

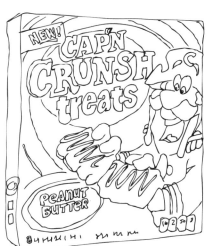

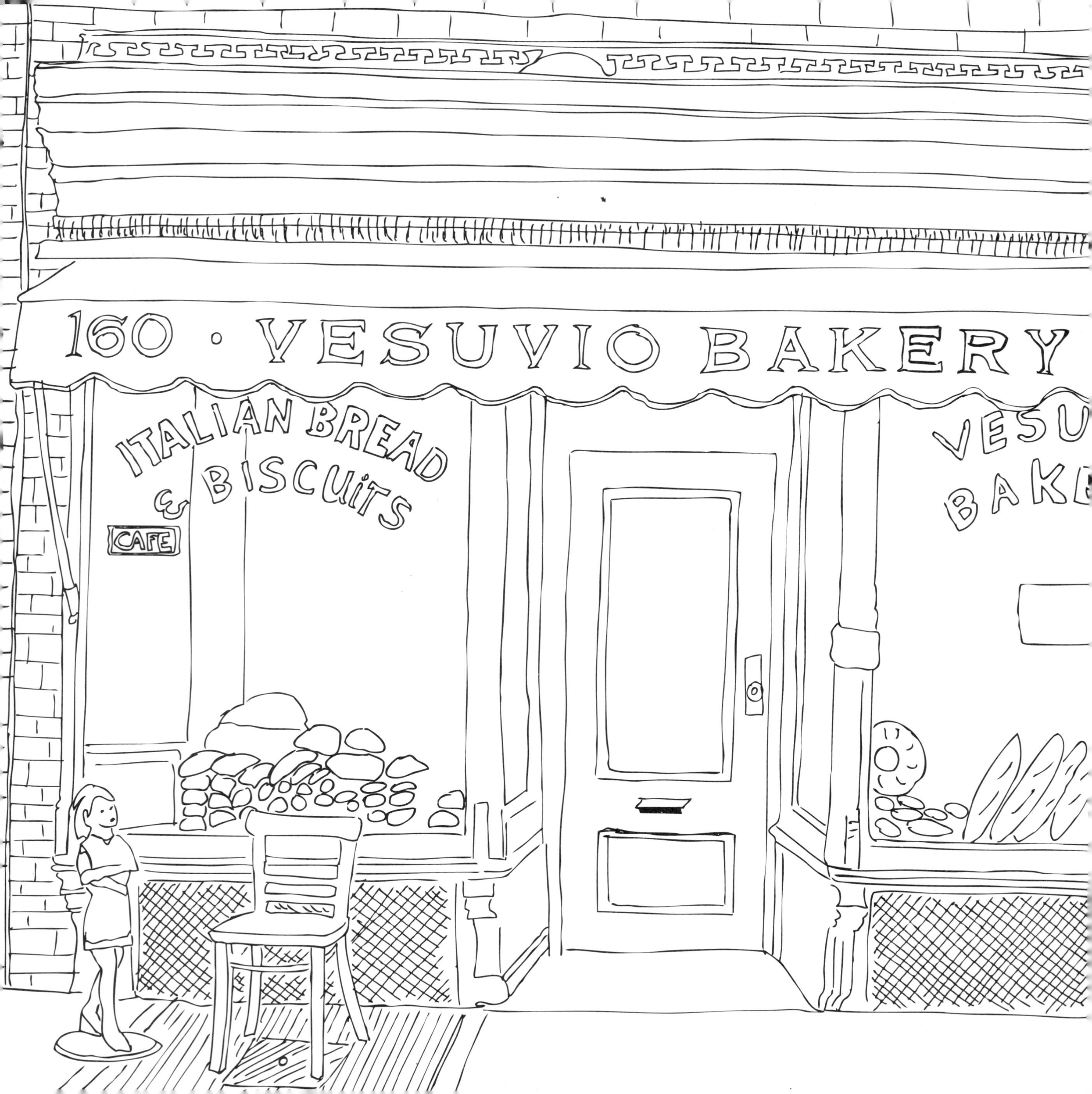
160 · VESUVIO BAKERY
ITALIAN BREAD
& BISCUITS
CAFE
VESU
BAKE

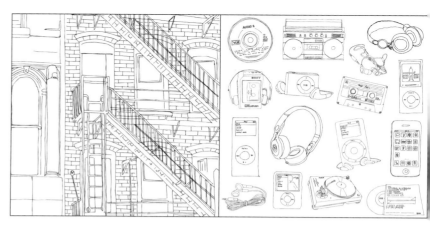

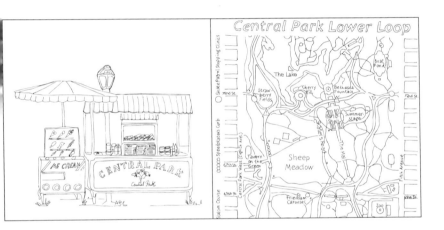

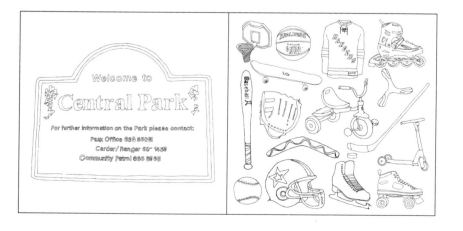

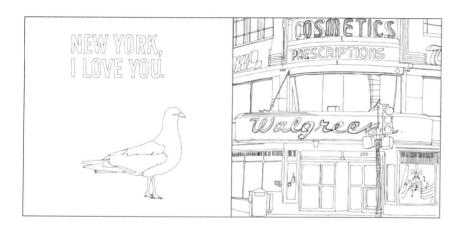

New York, I love you.

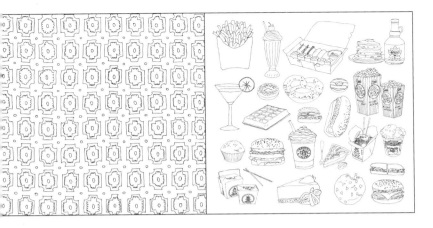

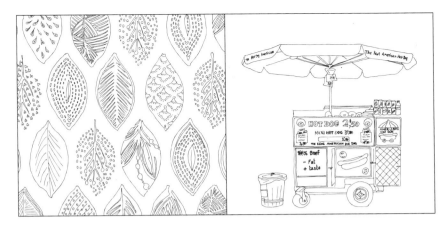